This Book Belongs To:

Published by Virgin 2009
2 4 6 8 10 9 7 5 3 1

The Magical World of Milligan © Spike Milligan Productions Limited, 2009
Introduction © Norma Farnes 2009

Condensed Animals © Spike Milligan Productions Ltd, 1991.
First published in Great Britain by Puffin Books.

Dip the Puppy © T.A. Milligan, 1974. First published in Great Britain by M. and J. Hobbs.

A Book of Bits © Spike Milligan, 1965. First published in Great Britain by Dennis Dobson Ltd.

Fleas, Knees and Hidden Elephants © Spike Milligan Productions Ltd, 1994.
First published in Great Britain by Boxtree.

A Mad Medley of Milligan © Spike Milligan Productions Ltd, 1999.
First published in Great Britain by Virgin Books.

A Dustbin of Milligan © Spike Milligan, 1961.
First published in Great Britain by Dobson Books Ltd.

Silly Verse for Kids © Spike Milligan, 1959. First published by Dennis Dobson Ltd.

The right of Spike Milligan to be identified as the author of this work
has been asserted by him under the Copyright, Designs and Patents Act 1988

First published in Great Britain in 2009 by
Virgin Books
Random House, 20 Vauxhall Bridge Road,
London SW1V 2SA

www.virginbooks.com
www.rbooks.co.uk

Cover design by Niki Charlton

Addresses for companies within The Random House Group Limited can be found at: www.randomhouse.co.uk/offices.htm

The Random House Group Limited Reg. No. 954009

A CIP catalogue record for this book
is available from the British Library

Hardback ISBN 9781905264841

The Random House Group Limited supports The Forest Stewardship Council [FSC], the leading international forest
certification organisation. All our titles that are printed on Greenpeace-approved FSC-certified paper carry the FSC logo.
Our paper procurement policy can be found at www.rbooks.co.uk/environment

Printed and bound China by C&C Offset Printing Co., Ltd.

The Magical World of Milligan

Stories & Poems

By
Spike Milligan

Edited by Norma Farnes

Contents

Introduction

Selecting and compiling this volume of children's poetry has been a joy. It brought back memories of the wonderful times Spike and I had and the laughter we shared. I remember my first day in the office. Spike was collating a selection of children's poems he had written, it was to be called *Milliganimals*. He read the first poem to me, 'Ant and Eleph-ant':

> Said a tiny Ant
> To the Elephant
> 'Mind how you tread in this clearing!'
>
> But alas! Cruel fate!
> She was crushed by the weight
> Of an Elephant, hard of hearing.

So my introduction to Spike was his love of children and animals. The year was 1966.

Many years later Spike said to me, 'I myself dote on children, and if you look closely you will find that most children are covered all over in dote marks. Don't worry: Persil will remove these dote marks and leave them smelling fresh-fresh dote marks. So please don't dote on children; it leaves them covered in marks – dote marks.'

It still makes me smile. His love of children and their innocence remained with him all his life.

In 1998 when 'On the Ning Nang Nong' was voted the nation's favourite poem, he wrote '1998 was a wonderful year for me. My poem "On the Ning Nang Nong" was voted the nation's favourite comic poem – now will they give me a knighthood?'

He got his wish. He was given an honorary knighthood in 2000, bestowed on him by someone he greatly admired: Prince Charles.

Norma Farnes

Condensed Animals

Ant

Little ant – little ant
Working all the day
Don't you ever want to go
Go outside and play?

Pouter pigeon

Puffery pouter pigeon
With your puffed-up chest
If I did that
My mum would make me
Go and wear a vest.

Mole

Mr Mole – Mr Mole
Burrowing under the green
It's no wonder – it's no wonder
That you're very rarely seen.

Bat

Bat bat bat bat
Flying in the night
Said my mum
When she saw one
It gave her quite a fright.

Toad

Toad toad
Little toad
Be careful how
You cross the road.

Skylark

Skylark skylark
Up high you sing your song
I want to know just how you stay
You stay up there so long.

Penguin

Penguin penguin
Sliding on the ice
Freezing your tootsies
Can't be very nice.

11

Horse

The horse of course
We like very much
Unless he kicks you
In the crutch.

Gorilla

Gorilla gorilla
I love gorillas
But not as Christmas
Stocking fillers.

Mule

He's half donkey
Half horse
He is in fact
A mule of course.

Stork

A stork will stand
On one leg all day
It's done to rest
The other they say.

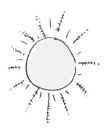

Glow-worm

Glow-worm glow-worm
With your flashing light
Yet they say at school
You're not very bright!

Aardvark

Aardvark aardvark
Living in Bolivia
Where the jaguars eat you
Wouldn't you rather live in 'ere?

Cow

The cow will give
A gentle moo
But that and milk
Is all she'll do.

Monkey

Monkey monkey
Pulling faces
Round and round
And round he races.
Up and down
In and out
What is that monkey
All about?

Eagle

Eagle eagle
In your eyrie
Flying up there
Must be weary.

Giraffe

A long neck
　　Has the giraffe
　　　He's a long way to go
　　　　To give a laugh.

Hyena

Hy-hy-hyena
In your jungle den
My advice to you is
Avoid hunting men.

Pussy-cat

Pussy-cat
What are vices?
Catching rats
And eating mices!

Elephant

Elephant elephant
Will you
Will you can't
Can you – can you
Elecant
Elecan
Elephant.

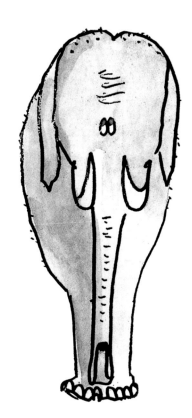

Owl

The owl at night
Without a light
His eyes can give you
Quite a fright.

Hippopotamus

Hip-po hip-po
Hippopotamus
Look at your big
Fat fat bottamus.

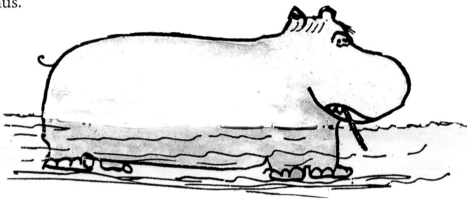

Orang-utan

The orang-utan
In a tree can hang
And seems quite happy that way – there
When the leaves turn brown
Some do come down
But they rarely ever stay – there.

Snail

Snail snail
Leaving a trail
Ugh! All slimy
From nose to tail.

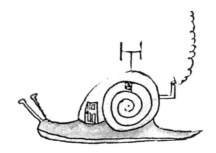

Frog

Frog frog
Jumping frog
He loves to live in
Swamp or bog
And whenever
Whenever he spoke
He went 'croak croak croak'.

Bee

Busy bee – busy bee
Making lots of honey
And from your work
You silly jerk
Someone else is making money.

Flea

Flea flea
Nipping me
Nipping where
I cannot see
Flea flea
Go away
I'm bitten on
My bum – I say!

Bug

A bug will bite
Your knees and nose
Nip you everywhere
He goes.

Fly

O fly – little fly
Whizzing whizzing
Whizzing by
Landing on my daddy's nose
On his head on his clothes
Little fly – whizz away
Had enough of you today.

Butterfly

Butterfly butterfly
Making colours in the sky
Red white and blue upon your wings
You are the loveliest of things.

Grasshopper

Grasshopper grasshopper
Making giant hops
In people's gardens
And the farmers' crops
Do be careful where you land
Little green grasshopper
Otherwise you understand
You may come a cropper.

Fish

Fish fish fish fish
In your coat of gold
You will get a lot of money
If you're bought or sold
If you ever sell your coat
Sell your coat of gold
You may get some money
But you'll be very cold.

Snake

Slithering slithering
Snake snake
Through the grass
By the lake
Mummy Mummy
Look at him
I never knew
A snake could swim!

Duck

Quack quack
Water just rolls
Off your back
Going quack quack
Quack quack quackers
You must drive your mummy crackers!

Cockerel

Cock-a-doodle-doo
Goes the cock
Every *every* morning at
Six o'clock
Wakes everybody
Up at dawning
Even on a
Sunday morning.

Cricket

Crick-crick-cricket
Sing your song
Singing singing
All night long
So dear cricket
Now instead
Instead of singing –
Off to bed.

Elephant

Elephant elephant
With your trunk so thin
That is what you use to let
The air get in.

Lamb

Baa-lamb baa-lamb
Crying for your mummy
Time for you to have some milk
From your mummy's tummy.

Chicken

Cluck cluck cluck
That's a chicken
Not a duck
So little hen
Listen to me then
All I beg
Is a nice big egg.

Pig

Pig pig
With your nose
You dig
Digging all
Your dinner out
Dig-dig-digging
With your snout.

Leopard

When you see a leopard
You'll see lots of spots
Dot dot dot dot
Dot dot dots!

Tortoise

Tortoise tortoise
Oh so slow
Although you start
You never seem to go.

Gnu

I knew – I knew
It's true – it's true
There's nothing new
About a gnu!

Salmon

Salmon salmon
In the River Tweed
You seem to swim
At such speed
And really salmon
How I wish
You wouldn't end up
On a dish.

Termite

Termite termite
The hes and shes might
Eat right through your bedroom floor
Eat the window – eat the door
Yet they never stop at that
They even eat poor Granny's hat!

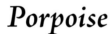

Porpoise

Porpoise you're a clever thing
Swim swim swim swimming
Stay in the sea – the sea is your song
Where you rightfully belong.

Sea-gull

The sea-gull lives by the sea-shore
And what's more
His favourite dish is
Little fishes.

Badger

Badger badger
In your set
Wish I had you
As a pet
But I bet
I bet I bet
You're very very
Hard to get.

Piranha

Piranha fishes – piranha fishes
Are very very very vicious
For the moment one dives in
They will strip off all your skin.

March hare

March hare – March hare
Mad as mad can be hare
But do do remember
He's much saner by September.

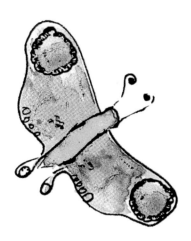

Moth

Moth moth
Like a piece of velvet cloth
You love the dark of night
But attracted by the light
Sometimes you burn on a candle's flame
Isn't that an awful shame?

Dragon-fly

Dragon-fly dragon-fly
Flying in the summer sky
Whizzing here – whizzing there
And you keep still in the air!

Whale

Whale whale
The size of your tail
Bring it down with a bash
It does sper-lash.

Wasp

Wasp wasp
With that sting in your tail
If you stuck it in me
I'd send you to jail.

Antelope

Antelope antelope
Over and over the plains you lope
You have lovely soft brown eyes
Just like Mr Bakewell pies.

Zebra

Zebra zebra black and white
Oh what a stunning sight
Like pyjamas on the run
Golly gosh what fun what fun.

Sea-lion

Sea-lion sea-lion
Playing in the waters
All together mums and dads
And their sons and daughters.

Tiger

Tiger tiger such a sight
Through the jungle in the night
Bet you're looking for your lunch
A tasty villager you can munch.

Alligator

Alligator alligator
How I hate him – how I hate her
The thought of swimming in your river
Really starts to make me shiver.

Hedgehog

Hedgehog hedgehog
Hedgehog in the garden
Makes snuffling snuffling noise
Please say 'Beg your pardon'.

Fox

Fox fox
Trying to catch a rabbit
Fox fox
What a nasty habit.

Water-buffalo

Water – water-buffalo
Into the water you go
Wallow wallow wallow wallow
Into every muddy hollow.

Swallow

Swallow swallow
Can I follow
You across the sea
If I did – I pray you bid
Please bring me back for tea.

Sea snake

Sea snake sea snake in the ocean
Swimming with that lovely motion
They say when you reach the shore
You wriggle off to Bangalore.

Kangaroo

Kangaroo kangaroo
Lamger-anage angeroo
Leaping leaping leapyloo
Bumpity-umpity-bumpity-boo.

Wart-hog

Wart-hog wart-hog
Are you ever caught hog?
You are very fat
No there's nothing wrong with that
But lions like you for their dinner
So you'd be much safer thinner.

Crow

The crow – the crow
Is black you know
Caw-caw-caw-cawing
Is very baw-baw-baw-bawring.

Chimpanzee

Chimp-chimp-chimpanzee
Some look like you and some like me
Mr Darwin clearly stated
That some time back we are related.

Toucan

Toucan toucan
You can – toucan
Rattle your beak
But you can't speak.

Jellyfish

Jellyfish jellyfish
Like a jelly on a dish
If I covered you with custard
You'd be very very flustered.

Seal

Seal seal
How does it feel
To swim in icy seas
Thank heavens your blubber
Is thick as rubber
Otherwise you'd freeze.

Ostrich

Ostrich with your skinny legs
Laying laying giant eggs
Never lay one for my tea
I couldn't eat it all you see.

Turtle

Turtle turtle
Heavy shell!
Yet you seem
To swim quite well.

Starfish

Starfish starfish
Lying on the bottom
You like eating litte bits
The moment that you spot 'em.

     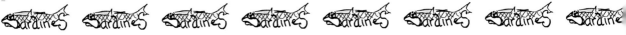

Sardine

Sardine sardine
These days you aren't often seen
The fishermen catch too many
Soon there won't be any.

Camel

Camel camel
Desert ship
You don't need water
On the trip.

Caterpillar

Caterpillar caterpillar
Passing by
Soon you'll be
A butterfly.

Skate

The skate is flat
Just like a mat
And that my fishy friend
Is that.

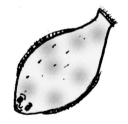

Rhinoceros

The rhinoceros
Is cross with us
'Cause someone's gone
And cut off his horn.

Highland deer

Highland deer – highland deer
I can hear your roars from here
See those antlers oh so grand
Just like my granny's old hat-stand.

Centipede

Centipede centipede
Over the ground you speed you speed
How many legs then have you got
Over a hundred – that's a lot.

Woodpecker

Woodpecker woodpecker
Pecking at the wood
At making holes in trees I'd say
You're very very good.

Tuna

Tuna tuna
I know you'd sooner
Not be in a tin
So please please please
You Japanese
Do not commit this sin.

Polecat

Polecat polecat
Whatever made you smell like that
You would really smell quite nice
Using aftershave Old Spice.

Worm

Slow worm – slow worm
Never on the go worm
Never never in a hurry
And I don't suppose you worry.

Bluebottle

Bluebottle bluebottle
You're a fly I'd like to throttle
Always landing on my food
Goodness gracious you're so rude!

Polar bear

Polar bear polar bear
In the Arctic Circle there
You were made a snowy white
So your camouflage is right.

Cockroach

Cockroach cockroach
You're a thing I won't approach
You're supposed to spread disease
As and when and where you please.

Kinkajou

Kinkajou kinkajou
I rarely ever think of you
I don't suppose you think of me
And that is how it's going to be.

Lizard

Lizard lizard
At scurrying you're a wizard
In and out the rocks you go
Like a little dynamo.

Millipede

Millipede millipede
Is very strange you see
He has to use a thousand legs
To get from A to B.

Cockatoo

Cockatoo cockatoo
Can I make a friend of you
If you don't want me as a friend
Make your crest stand up on end.

Wolf

Wolf wolf in the snow
Hunting hunting off you go
The finest meal there is for you
Is a nice fat caribou.

Sea-horse

Sea-horse sea-horse
You can't gallop of course
But you have a pair of wings
Sea-horses are the strangest things.

Mongoose

Mongoose mongoose
You can frighten snakes
Mongoose – strongoose
Think of the courage it takes.

Yak

The yak – the yak
Will rarely attack
It's a docile little beast
Will not harm you in the least.

Otter

Otter otter in a stream
You've a life of which I dream
Frolicking the livelong day
Living just to fish and play.

Pretty Polly

Pretty Polly pretty Polly
In the apple tree with your scarlet beak
Eating all the apples up never mind the squawking
Please save one for me let us hear you *speak*!

Ostrich

Ostrich you're a funny bird
People say you look absurd
Others say you look a mess
With your lack of gracefulness.

Albatross

Albatross albatross
All the oceans you must cross
Yet you never seem to land
That's something I can't understand.

Budgerigar

Budgerigar budgerigar
What a chatterbox you are
My aunty loves it when
You say, 'Who's a pretty boy, then?'

Octopus

Octopus with legs a-gate
Count them and
They come to eight.

Reindeer

Reindeer in the snowy waste
Have to jolly well make haste
For speed the wolf can match him
And therefore can often catch him.

Gazelle

Thomson's gazelle
Can run like hell
So though he bought one
He's never caught one.

Boar

Boar boar – wild boar
Eating off the forest floor
You grunt and grunt when you eat food
My mummy says that's very rude.

Lobster

Lobster lobster in the sea
Locked up in your armoury
Just like an ancient knight of old
Except you're very very cold.

Krill

Krill krill – multifarious krill
Great clouds and clouds of you just like swill
The sad part of this tale I tell 'ee
They all end up inside a whale's belly.

Locust

Hear the warning
Locust swarming
Eating everything that's green
Look there goes my runner bean.

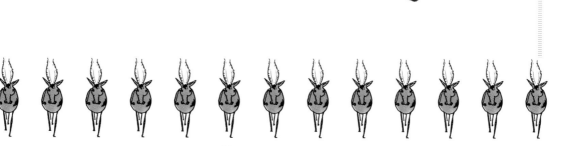

Dip the Puppy

There was once a mummy dog, her name was Pom-Pom and she had 3 baby puppies, one black, called Splot, one brown, called Bing, and a white one called Dip. Splot and Bing could both go "Bow wow, woof woof", but poor Dip went "Meiow meiow" like a pussy cat! "What's the matter with you Dip?" said his mummy "dogs dont go Meiow", so Dip tried again but he still went "Meiow" and all the other doggies all laughed at Dip, poor little Dip was very sad. For 2 weeks he tried to go "Bow wow" but every time, he went "Meiow". Every

one made fun of little Dip, so one
night, Dip ran away from home, he
crept out the back door and went and
hid in the woods. It was very dark
and cold and a big storm came and
it started to rain, Dip got wet and
cold, he sat on the ground and cried,
just then a snail rushed up at 50
miles a year; "Look out puppy! you're
right in the middle of a very busy snail
road, you better be careful theres another snail rushing by here any year now!"
Dip said "Please do you know some where
I can sleep? The snail said "Yes" and he
took Dip to a hole in the ground (Big Deal!)
and shouted "Anyone in? Up popped a

pink spotted rabbit wearing glasses "My name is Nibbles" he said "Can this puppy sleep in your den tonight?" said snail "Yes, as long as he hasn't got any fleas" said Nibbles, so down the hole went Dip and they came to a lovely little rabbits room, on the floor was nice clean straw and grass and it was warm and cosy. Nibbles gave Dip some carrots and mushrooms, then Nibbles played the banjo and sang furry songs

I am a funny Rabbit,
I'm pink with spots of red,
But now my ears are tired,
So, I think I'll go to bed.

"Do you know any songs Dip?" said Nibbles.
"Yes I do" said Dip who stood on a chair

and sang

Oh there was a little boy
His name was Jimmy Brown
But everytime he gave a sneeze
His trousers they fell down!

They both laughed and went to bed in the straw. Next morning Nibbles woke Dip up with a nice cup of tea and some nuts. "Where are you going now?" said Nibbles, who was combing his ears. "I don't know" said Dip "I've run away from home because I can't bark like a doggie, I keep going meiow". Nibbles said " Oh dear, that's very serious, but I know a flying fox called Flip-flap who can help you". Off they went and they came to an old ruined church, and hanging upside down from inside the roof was Flip-flap and he was singing an upside down song

I'm singing hanging upside down
Some people think I'm silly
But that's how God has made me
So I'm not a silly Billy

When he saw Dip he said "Well, what do you want, hurry up or I'll put a flea on your tail?" So Dip told him he couldn't bark. "Ah!" said Flip-flap "I know a great Wizard called Mr Sloppy-knickers who might help you, but he lives a long way away on top of a mountain, and you have to cross a river full of crocodiles, so be very, very

careful". Dip said he was frightened to go on his own. "I'll come with you and be your friend" said Nibbles. So Dip and Nibbles started on their long journey. First they came to a great sandy desert, and the sun was so hot if you touched a rock it burnt you, and it would melt your chocolate. "Oh dear I'm so thirsty" said Dip "If we don't get some water soon we'll die of thirsty. Just then they saw a beautiful green and yellow snake going along and it said "Sssss, if you want some water follow me," but he went so fast they had to run to keep up with him. The snake took them to some big rocks and coming out of one was a lovely stream of cool water!

Dip and Nibbles drank and drank until they
had big fat tummies. They said goodbye
to the snake and went on to look for
the wizard; in the evening they came to
a singing mountain.

I am a rocky mountain
And children climb up me
When they get to the top
They have to stop
Cause theres no more up you see!

A little way up they found a cave, "Let's
sleep in here to-night" said Dip, so they
got some grass and straw and made 2
little beds, and Nibbles made a fire and
Dip got some black berries and some
apples; after they had eaten them they

74

snuggled down in their little beds. In the middle of the night some savages came in to the cave, they grabbed Dip and Nibbles and tied them up. "Help! Help" shouted Dip "Keep quiet" said a savage "or we'll cut off your tail". They took poor Dip and Nibbles to the King of the Savages, he was a big fat black man; he was wearing a tin top hat and a grass skirt, his name was King Blackbottom. When he saw Dip and Nibbles he said "Oh yum-yum, I'll have you for dinner to-morrow"; they took Dip and Nibbles and locked them in a straw hut in the dark. "What are we going to do Nibbles? said Dip. "I've got sharp teeth and I'm going to nibble a hole in this straw wall" and he nibbled

and nibbled and he made a big hole and
Nibbles and Dip crept out and ran till they
were a long way from the savages but!
they could hear the savages following
them again, Dip saw a tree with a hole in.
"Lets hide in there" he said, so they both
squeezed into the hole, and only just in time,
because just then the savages came by.
Their King was shouting "Find them, I want
that puppy for my dinner, Ill eat him with
peanut butter; but they didnt find them,
and after a while they went away.
"Thank heavens they've gone, I was so
frightened" said Dip. "Come on, lets get
on" said Nibbles. They walked all day and
in the evening they came to a big river.

There was no bridge, so they couldn't get across "Look" said Nibbles "there are some ropes going across the river over there so they started to cross the river on the ropes but they did'nt know that the ropes were really the strands of a giant spiders web; when Nibbles and Dip were half way across, a giant red spider came out of a hole and was creeping towards them. "Look out!" shouted Nibbles. "What shall we do?" said Dip, "We'll have to fall in the river", so they let go and Splash! Splash! fell in the river and started to swim to the side. Dip got out first and then he saw a crocodile coming up behind Nibbles, and he was just going to bite off his tail when Kerbonkkk! Dip hit the crocodile on his head with a big stone. "Owww! I've gone all giddy" said crocodile, "and my eyes are going blink-blink-blinkety-blink and the buttons have fallen off my socks", and off he went to the lump-on-the-head doctor. Nibbles got out of the water. "Thank you for saving my tail Dip, you see, if a bunny loses his tail his ears go green". As they were talking along came a man paddling a pink canoe full of little white mice. "They keep the cats away" he said, "my name is John Ticklesock". "Can you give us a lift mister?" said Nibbles. "Yes yes yes yes yes yes" said

John "some people like ice lollies, I like to say yes yes yes yes". Away down the river they all went "I'm a banana hunter" said John "How do you do that?" said Diß "Well, I creeß up on them at night when the bananas are asleeß, and I catch them before they run away" Diß laughed "I've never seen bananas running, he said, "Thats because they're always asleeß" said John. "You're a funny man, laughed Nibbles. "Well, I'd rather eat bananas than eat animules", said John. Soon they came to a big sloßßy horse wearing a Yellow toß hat and white boots; on his belly was written 'I'm going to Sloßßy Knickers' house free', so Diß and Nibbles

JOHN TICKLESOCK THE HUNTER

said 'Good bye John Jicklesock", and rode away
on the big sloppy horse whos name was Clop'.
and he sang a song

     I'm a horse

     I'm a horse

     Of <u>course</u> I'm a horse

     I dont know how

     To be a cat

     Dog or Cow,

     And so I'll stay

     a horse that goes neigh.

"I used to go quack", said the horse, "but the
Wizard cured me", Dip felt very happy, soon
he would be able to go Woof Woof like all
the other dogs at school. Up and up a big
hill they went, along a road that kept

'CLOP'
the
Sloppy Horse.

going Oh! ouch! Oww' Dib asked Clob why the road was making such a noise "Its because he doesn't like people walking on him;" "If a horse walked on me I'd go oh! ouch! as well" said Nibbles; the road made such a noise shouting "Get your big horse boots off me!" they had to walk on the grass. At the top of the hill they saw the Wizard's house. "Hooray! said Dib, "Yarooh" said Nibbles, which was Hooray Backwards. The Wizards house was made of thousands of different coloured pieces of glass, and shone like a million rainbows, it was like all the butterflies' wings in the world joined together and the sun shining on them. "Its nearly as pretty

One of the Woolly Monkeys Playing the Piano

as my mummy's face" said Diß, "but not like dad's big red spotty conk". From inside the house they heard strange music, Tinkle-inkle-plinkel-splash! it went "It sounds like some one dropping knives and forks down the toilet"! said Nißßles, Cloß the horse laughed "Hur-Hur-Hur--what-a-silly-boo-I-am-Hur-Her-Heee", but he had to stop because his false teeth fell out and went 'Dongg! on a smelly old Pussy Cats tail "Help-meiow! said pussy and shot up in the air and went to sleep on the moon where there were no horses teeth, only green sausages that went "Pee-Pippety-Pee-Bonk! The Wizard's house had <u>ten</u> front doors, all different

Frozen Fred
the talking ICE
LOLLY

SM

sizes. "Number 8 is the right size door for us" said Nibbles, but I'll have to bend my ears down". Dip rang the door bell and it went "Blu- blu- blu- blu-blu; blu"! "Its a blue-bell" said Dip. The door opened and there was a Red Ice Lolly with one leg in a big yellow boot. "I'm Frozen Fred" he said "Follow me", and off he hopped down a long hall full of flowers, and bright blue and lemon parrots wearing spotted socks! they went past two hundred woolly monkeys called Edward Heath [spinster] all playing pianos, then they came to a giant room made from silver paper, in the middle was a pond with a

THE MAGICIAN MR SLOPPY KNICKERS

Fountain squirting lemonade up a
Policeman's trousers. "It keeps my old
Knobbley legs nice and cool" he said;
then he blew his whistle "Wheee-Wheee"
and out came three fatty-boo Penguins
One with a trumpet!
One with a drum !!
And one with a pancake,
Stuck to his bum!
Then into the room came Mr Sloppy-
knickers, he had snow white hippy
hair, a long beard and Donny Osmond's
shirt, with biscuits for buttons and
he was blowing bubbles from his ear!
Frozen Fred said "This puppy can't go
Woof Woof;" The Wizard picked up

ONE OF THE Penguins PLAYING THE
TRUMPET.

(SM)

Dip and carried him down a long staircase that went under the ground; along the walls hung apples, oranges, pears and omelets hanging on nails, and lots of other food "It's in case I get hungry" said Mr Sloppy-knickers, and he gave Dip a nice banana with a zip fastener on it, and he gave to Nibbles, a chocolate carrot from Hong-Kong. At the bottom of the stairs, instead of a floor, there was <u>water!</u> "Come on" said Mr Sloppy-knickers and <u>stood</u> on the <u>water!</u> "Help, we can't do that" said Nibbles, but the Wizard picked them up and put them on the water and they didn't sink. "Yarooh! said

Dip, [which was Hooray backwards] we can walk on the water! how did you learn this trick?"

"From a man called Jesus, he's the goodest Wizard of all"! They ran along the top of the water singing, soon they came to a big purple door, the Wizard opened it, and inside were hundreds of pussy-cats having a dance and singing meiow-meiow songs; as soon as Dip saw them he went

"Grrr - Woof Woof. Bow-wow-woW!
"Did you hear that?" said Nibbles "you barked like a real doggie, you're cured"!
"Oh yaro" said Dip [which was Hooray sideways] thank you Mr Sloppy-knickers"!

The Wizard told Dip "That will cost you fifty pence." Dip felt in his pocket, "I've only got one p" he said. "Then you'll have to give it to me fifty times" said Sloppy-knickers. After this, they had a super tea party where 600 frogs sang "God Save the Queen and God help Princess Anne", then on came all the school teachers wearing droopy-drawers and they did a dance and splosh! some one threw a custard pie right in a teachers face!!! Dip laughed so much his tail went straight. "Its time to go back home" said Nibbles. The Wizard said "You can ride back on my flying bugle." so on they climbed, and, Woosh!

up they went, over the moon where they saw some silly men picking up rocks. "They're barmy" said Nibbles "I know" said Dip, and sang a song:

Hooray for Sloppy-knickers
Who stopped me going Meiow
And now like all my brothers
I'll always go Bow-wow.

Soon Dip was back with his mummy, daddy and his brothers, they all got into a nice warm bath, and shampooed their tails so they were nice and clean for dinner time, when they had fish fingers and fish toes and they all lived happily ever-after until breakfast time.

A Book of Bits

A Special Guest Appearance of Eric Sykes

You cannot hear what he is playing as this is a silent film.

Coat of Arms

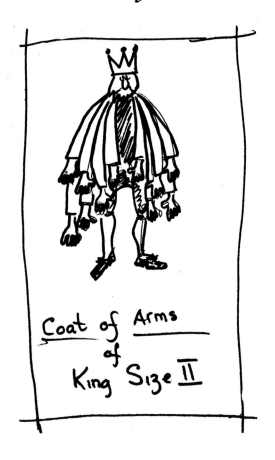

Coat of Arms
of
King Size II

Great Feets of Strength

Casabazonka

The boy stood on
    the burning deck
Whence all but
    he had fled –
        Twit.

Ancient Chinese Song

Itchy Dingle Dangle
Dingle Dangle Doo,
Going once!
Going twice!
Sold! To Fu Manchu!

Chorus: etc., etc.

A Poem Called
Sophia Loren of Leeds

Ingle Jingle
Jangle Jom
Tingle Ingle
Dangle Dom
Fringle Frangle
Bangle Bom!
And there's more, my friend,
Where that came from!!

The Prayer of the Civil Servant

When it's OBE time in England
And the knighthoods flow like wine,
In next year's Birthday Honours
If you're stuck for a name, use mine.

Chorus: Rule Britannia, *etc., etc.*

Malice at Buckingham Palace

Outside Buckingham Palace
  a dog was barking one day
When out of a house
  came a chocolate mouse
And frightened that doggie away.

And so that chocolate mousie
  was taken to the Queen—
Who swallowed him up
  with a gobbledy glup.
I do think that was mean.

Chorus: Here's a health unto her Majesty, *etc., etc.*

The Skate

'Tis sad to relate
That skate cannot skate!
In the sea, they lie on the bottom.
They lie quite still
In waters chill
Until a fisherman's got 'em!

A very sad fate
for non-skating skate.

Genuine Skating Fish

Deep-frozen Skate

Chorus: Rule Britannia, *etc., etc.*

Eels

Eileen Carrol
Had a barrel
Filled with writhing eels
And just for fun
She swallowed one:
Now she knows how it feels.

Chorus: Rule Britannia, *etc., etc.*

My Happily Splashing Daughter

My happily splashing daughter
Said, "My legs are getting shorter!"
Well she must be dim
To go for a swim
In that shark-ridden water!

When I Get Hot

When I get hot
They say I've got
A temperature or flu:
If I go red ~~flu~~
I'm put to bed
With an Aspro in or two.
And in this state
I lie and wait
Until they say I'm better
Then as a rule
Sent back to school
With an explanation letter

The Dreaded Tootsie-Kana

When the Tootsie-Kana comes,
Hide yourself behind your thumbs;
Tie a dustbin on your head;
Stay indoors; go to bed.

When the Tootsie-Kana goes,
Peel an apple with your toes;
Buy a sausage; paint it red—
Tootsie-kana falls down dead.

Chorus: 'Twas Blollig and the Schalomey
Touves did gear and grumble in
the Wardrobe, *etc., etc.*

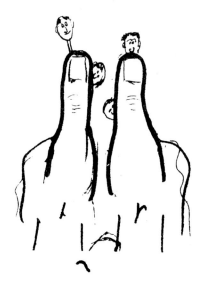

Holy Smoke

I am the Vicar of St Paul's
And I'm ringing the steeple bell,
The floor of the church is on fire,
Or the lid has come off hell.

Shall I ring the fire brigade?
Or should I trust in the Lord?
Oh dear! I've just remembered,
I don't think we're insured!

"What's this then?" said the fire chief.
"Is this church C of E?
It is? Then we can't put it out,
My lads are all R.C.!"

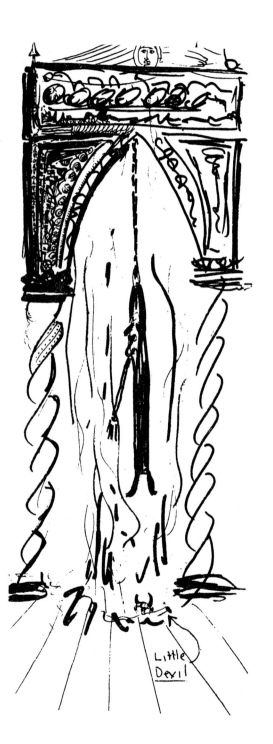

Little Devil

Twit Bits

Hairy Wading Twitts

HAIRY WADING TWITTS.

Plucked Hairee Twyt

Hairless Cluck

PLUCKED HAIRES. TWYT

Long-necked hairee

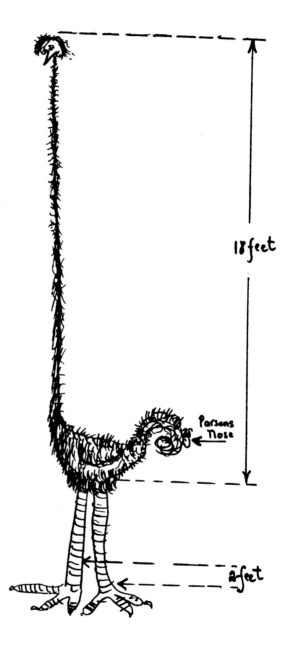

18 feet

Parsons
Nose

2 feet

Permanently grounded flightless twitt bird

Adopted as national emblem for Concorde plane project

DUTCH HELICOPTER.

HOOVER

Knownothing twit birds

usually seen on first nights

Little Scots-kilted hairee

Scots spider

owned by Robert Bruce

Suspicious Twitt

The suspicious twitt
Has a hard time of it.
He has one major fear—
An attack from the rear!
So he perpetually revolves his head
To avoid being killed (dead).
He'll finally die a corkscrewed wreck,
Killed by a heavily twisted neck.

Chorus: Good-bye, little yellow bird, *etc., etc.*

Contented Little Caged Hairee Twit

A bird in a cage
Puts all heaven in a rage!
But not the contented twit,
He doesn't mind a bit.

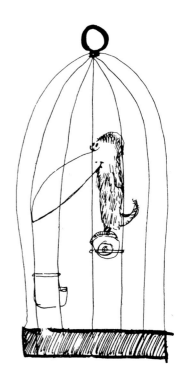

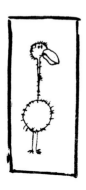

Little Insignificant Twit

The little insignificant twit bird
Is very seldom seen or heard.
There's never been a pair, I fear,
So how the devil did he get here?

Insecure Trouser-Nesting Hairee

You've probably never heard
Of the trouser-nesting bird.
He lives on tops of houses
And wears his nest like trousers.

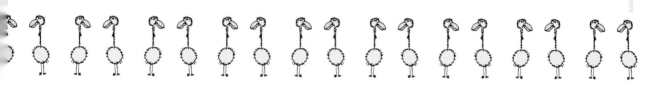

The Heraldic Twit Eagle

The Heraldic Twit Eagle
Is far from being regal
But he fills in the fields
On armorial shields
And during a joust
He gets hit foust.*

*First

Go North, South, East and West, Young Man

Drake is going West, lads,
So Tom is going East;
But tiny Fred
Just lies in bed,
The lazy little beast.

Chorus: Drake is going, *etc., etc.*

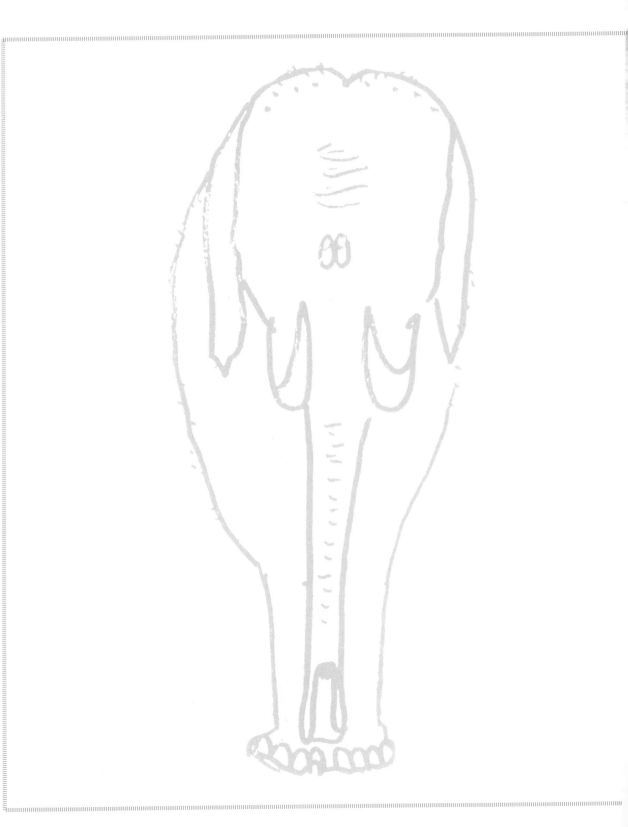

Fleas, Knees and Hidden Elephants

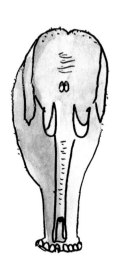

Timothy Nerp

Timothy Nerp was a terrible Twerp
A terrible Twerp was he
He wore his trousers back to front
To keep out the raging sea
He wore his socks both inside out
To stop the rising damp
He filled his boots with mustard
To stop the dreaded cramp
He wore his trilby upside down
To try and catch the rain
Then every day at half past one
He'd start all over again.

Skin Deep

I think that I am lovely
Despite a broken nose
You can detract from it
By wearing fancy clothes
I think I am beautiful
Although I have cross-eyes
You can detract from that as well
By wearing fancy ties
I think I am beautiful
Even though I've got big ears
I cover them with blankets
When anyone appears.
I think I am beautiful
Although my legs are thin
If people want to see them
I say my legs aren't in
If some folk say I'm ugly
As some folk certainly will
I get out my rotweiler
And say kill kill kill

Hidden Elephant

Splitty splitty splat!
What was that?
Splitty splitty splat!
Was it a rat?
Can a rat go splitty splitty splat?
No! Then can a cat?
No! Cats only go miaow
Don't ask me how
Can a cow go splitty splitty splat?
No cows go moo
That's what they do
Splitty splitty splat!
Heavens! It's somewhere in my flat!
Got it! It's an elephant under my hat!

Trousers

Somehow my trousers have got bent
Right in the middle there's a dent
I tried to straighten them on the
floor
But somehow they ended up next
door
I went for a walk with these
trousers bent
They took me to a place in
Kent
With my trousers back
to front, away I darted
Only to end up where
I started.

Terence Blatt

Terence Blatt
Wore bells on his hat
To keep the wolves at bay
With a gun by his side
He went for a ride
In his one horse open sleigh
A wolf pursued him
As snow began to fall
It ate him up bells and all
Oh dear Terence what terrible luck
The wolf of course didn't give a fig

The Dancer

He danced with a monkey
He danced with a cat
And he danced with a man
In a big black hat
He danced with a Muslim
He danced with a Jew
And he danced with a Chinaman
Six foot two
Then he took all his clothes off
And he danced all day
That's when they came
And took him away.

Tiger

There came a tiger trailing me
So I climbed up a banana tree
The tiger wouldn't go away
So, where I was, I had to stay
I threw a banana on his head
Lo and behold, it struck him dead.
So if you don't want to come to any harmer
Always carry a spare banana.

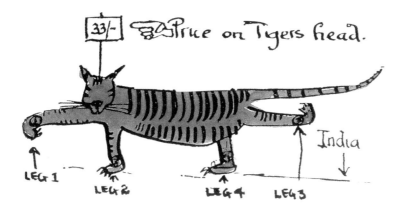

Tiger

I'm hunting for a tiger skin
Here's the jungle, I go in
Into view the tiger came
So very carefully, I took aim
The tiger gave a sudden cough
And when he did, his stripes fell off.

Piffed

I piffed at my mother
I piffed at my dad
'Will you stop that piffing
It's driving us mad!'
I piffed at my mistress
The next day at school
I piffed and I piffed
The silly old fool.
I piffed at Willy
I piffed at Bert
And I piffed at the tail
On my grandad's shirt
Oh I piffed and I piffed
Oh I piffed everywhere.
Then I piffed at the Queen
So there – so there.

THE QUEEN WAS HERE

The Hills Are Alive

Climb every mountain
Ford every stream
Follow every rainbow
Till you find you're knackered.

Never Never

Never force cats to wear hats
It'll stop them catching rats
Never put a dog in trousers
It could stop them guarding our houses
You must never put a duck in slacks
It would surely stop his flow of quacks
Never force a goose into a gown
It would only go honk and then drown.
You must never cross a chicken's leg
Unless you want some funny shaped eggs
Never put a monicle on a rooster
Or he will think he's Bertie Wooster
These are things you mustn't do
Now off to the vets with all of you.

The Dali Lama

The Dali Lama
Wore half a pyjama
When he went to bed
The other half
He ate for a laugh
And this disease could spread

The Dali Lama
Wore half a pyjama
Red and white and blue
The other half
He burnt on a staff
Now this would never do

The Dali Lama
Wore half a pyjama
Eating jam and bread
The other half
He fed to a calf
He's getting no better, they said.

The Donkey

Hee-haw said the donkey
He who said the mule
He me said the donkey
That's who you silly fool.

Child's Prayer

Can you hear me God?
Can you? Can you?
Do you have big ears God
Do you? Do you?
Do they help you listen in
Or is it because the walls are thin
What's it like being God
Does it make you ever feel odd
Up there can you get apple-pie
How can you eat it up so high
Please can I see you God
Only just a peep!
If you're not here by 8 o'clock
I'm going off to sleep

My Love and I

My love and I
A-wickling go
Whickle whackle woo

My love and I
A-wickling went
Tickle Ickle too

My love and I
A-wickling did
Bickle backle biff

My love and I
Wickled away
And both fell over a cliff

Big Head

My name is Fred
I've got a big head
With my head on the pillow
It collapses the bed
One day I went to buy a hat
The man said help!
We could never fit that
So now when I go out of doors
On my head I wear a chest of drawers
If I want to see what's behind or before
I throw out the clothes and open a drawer

Ponk a Loo

It's a Ponk a Loo – ho Ponk a Loo
That's the thing the Chinese do
They go Ponk a Loo out doors
And sometimes on the bathroom floors
They say it causes no offence
But difficult when crowds are dense
So Ponk a Loo Ponk a Loo
The Chinese do it – why don't you?

Il Papa

The pope arose at 6pm
And said his morning prayer
When he'd had his breakfast
He said another there
Then just before shaving
He blessed his razor blade
Then a prayer of hope
For his shaving soap
And the place where it was made
Then he prayed to St Theresa
To straighten the Tower of Pisa
While wearing his white fur capel
He blessed the Sistine Chapel
When saying grace before meals
He fell backwards head over heels
He said you see my dearest God
You made me such a clumsy sod.

The Purtakon

See there the Purtakon
See the slender girth
And the scarlet yondel
Grown like that since birth.
See how the Purtakon
Goes gargle-argle goo
Best stand back
Or he'll attack
And squirt it over you.

Now hear how the Purtakon
Is making such a din
I'll have to shout
Let's all get out!
The way that we got in.

Knees (song)

You've got to have knees
You've got to have knees
They're the things that take stock when
you sneeze
You've got to have knees
You've got to have knees
They only come in twos but never threes
You've got to have knees
You've got to have knees
In the winter fill them up with anti-freeze
You've got to have knees
You've got to have knees
Famous for having them are bees
You've got to have knees
You've got to have knees
If you want to see mine, say please
You've got to have knees
You've got to have knees
They help you run away from falling
trees
Knees. Wonderful knees!

The Lion

If you're attacked by a lion,
Find fresh underpants to try on.
Lay on the ground, keep quite still,
Pretend that you are very ill
Keep like that, day after day
Perhaps the lion will go away.

Donkey

Do not touch that donkey, mam
Mam I'm warning you
That donkey has a disease
Called Itchy dangle do
If you touch that donkey mam
You'll start to go bright green
Even reaching parts of you
That you have never seen
So then my dear madam
A warning to the few
If you get near that donkey
He'll do it over you.

The Leg

The other day I gave a cough
There and then my leg fell off
A policeman gave it a stamp
And said 'You cannot leave it there'
I took it to the doctor who said
I'm sorry but this leg is dead
I was shocked into grieving
Then I heard the leg still breathing!
When I knew it wasn't dead
I rushed it to a hospital bed
It was stitched back on by Doctor Hay
But facing, alas, the other way
Now when I walk I have found
I only go around and around.

Horses

Horses for courses
Who said that?
He must be talking
Through his hat
A horse is something
I never ate
First it wouldn't fit
On the plate.
Supposing, it was
Under done
He'd give a snort
And away he'd run.
Leaving you with
Just potatoes and peas
Not much of a meal
If you please
What was supposed to be your dinner.
Could be next year's
Derby Winner.

The Terrible Monster Jelly

Once upon a time, a hundred and wobbley years ago, in a town called Mdina, on the island of Malta, there lived a family, a Mummy and Daddy and two children, a boy called Peepo and a girl called Maria. The town was surrounded by big fortress walls so no-one could get in except through the one big main gate. Outside of the town lived lots of families who all worked on farms. The farms all belonged to a wicked and cruel king who lived in a Palace in Mdina. He made all the farmers and their children work very hard from early in the morning to late at night. He only gave them a little money, and if any of them became sick, he would not let them see a doctor, or go to bed, and sometimes the sick people died. So all the mummys, daddys and their children were very sad, and very hungry. The King had plenty of money and food, and he was very greedy; Peepo and Maria's daddy worked as a cook in the King's kitchen. He was a very good cook and could make lovely cakes and puddings and bright coloured jellies, but the King was always cruel to Daddy. The King would say 'This jelly is too small, I want a bigger one,' and he would throw the jelly on the floor, where his dogs would eat it all up. So poor Daddy would go back to the kitchen and make a *bigger* jelly, and then the King would eat it all up and say, 'I'm *still* hungry, make a bigger one quickly, or I will chop your head off.' So poor Daddy worked all night and made a big jelly as big as a chair, but the wicked King ate it all up Gibble Gobble, Gibble Gobble, Swallow, Swallow, Glup!

Then he said 'I'm *still hungry*, if by tomorrow evening you haven't made me a bigger jelly, I will put both your children in a dark underground prison till they die!' When Daddy went home and told the family they were all very frightened and the Mummy started to cry. The Daddy said 'I don't know *how* to make a bigger jelly.' When the children went to bed they said prayers, 'Please God help us and stop the wicked King putting us in prison,' then they went to sleep.

Early in the morning when it was still asleep-time there was a *tap-tappity-tap* on the window. 'Wake up!' said Maria to Peepo. They got up and went to the window, and there outside was a beautiful little angel-fairy. She was only as big as a thimble and she was holding a tiny jelly on a plate. The children opened the window and let her in. 'Who are you?' said the children. 'I am Saint Chivers. God heard you praying for help and He sent me with this jelly for the King.' 'That's too small for the wicked King,' said Peepo. 'He wants a giant jelly.'

'Don't worry,' said Saint Chivers, 'this is a magic jelly. You keep it and give it to the King tomorrow and you will see how it is a magic jelly' and the angel-fairy flew away. The children went back to sleep. When they woke up again they saw that the little jelly had got *bigger*. 'Oh, we'll have to put it on a bigger plate.' They rushed downstairs and told their Mummy and Daddy about the magic jelly and what the angel-fairy had said. They all ran upstairs with a bigger plate but the jelly had got too big for the second plate, so they took the magic jelly downstairs and put it on a bigger plate, but it was still getting bigger and bigger, so Daddy said 'I'll put it in a big bucket.' When he had done this he ran to the King's Palace, and the jelly was bigger still, so he put it on a big round table. The King was shouting 'Hurry up! I want my jelly.' The jelly was now as big as a window and Daddy had to get three men to help him carry the magic jelly to the King's dinner table. When the King saw the jelly it was as high as a door, but even *then* he wasn't satisfied, 'It's still too small, as soon as I've eaten it up, with a Gobbledy Glup, I'm going to throw you, your wife, and your children into a deep dark prison full of snakes and mud!' Two soldiers grabbed poor Daddy and tied him up. 'Go and bring his wife and children here and tie them up too,' said the wicked King. Then the King started to eat the magic jelly.

'Oh yum-yum-yummummy
I've got jelly in my tummy!'

The King Full of Jelly!

he said. He sat eating for over one hour. 'That's funny,' said the wicked King, 'the jelly hasn't got smaller.' By now the guards had brought back Mummy and the two children, all tied up with chains. They watched as the King tried to eat all the magic jelly but, no, he couldn't, the jelly was getting bigger and bigger – and people started to laugh – the King was so angry. The jelly was now half as big as the room so they had to take it out in the garden, then it got as big as the garden and the king was still trying to eat it as fast as he could. 'Eat-Eat-fast-Eat' he went but the jelly got as big as the garden, so they had to carry it out into the street.

By now the King had eaten so much jelly he was as fat as a house, all his trousers had split open and showed his bare bottom, everybody was laughing at him and he was so angry he started to cry. Still the jelly got bigger and bigger – so he made the people carry it into the Park, and then he had eaten so much he was so full of jelly his tummy was like a big big round ball and he fell over and rolled down the street, through the gate out into the fields where all the poor people were working. The magic jelly was getting bigger than the Park. 'Someone help me,' screamed the King, 'if someone doesn't eat it all, that jelly will fill the whole city and my Palace will be *inside* the jelly.' Just then, the soldiers came down the road with their prisoners and Peepo and Maria said to the King, 'If we get rid of the jelly, will you promise to be kind and give plenty of food to the poor people?'

'Oh yes, I promise,' said the King, 'and I'll never be bad again.' So the soldiers released Peepo and Maria who got all the poor children together and said, 'Who likes jelly?' and all the poor hungry children said, 'We do.' So they all marched to the King's Palace; they each got a spoon from the kitchen, and they went to the Park and started to eat the Giant Jelly, and they were *so* hungry they ate it all up in twenty minutes, three seconds – a world record for eating jellies.

Then they all sang –

Yuma-Yuma-Yummy
We've got jelly in our tummy
Now we'll all go home
To Daddy and Mummy

The King was so pleased he gave each family a hundred gold and silver coins, and all the children a gold spoon with their name on it, and he was never cruel any more, and they all lived happily until the next jelly.

A Mad Medley of Milligan

How

My father was an Elephant
My mother was a Cow
How I got here
I don't know how

Van Gogh

With hand signals
And a polite cough
He bid twelve million
For a Vincent Van Gogh
For that sort of money
I'd cut my right ear off

Something

I saw a piece of something
What it was I cannot say
You see that piece of something
Was going the other way
Suddenly that piece of something
Turned round and back again
I just couldn't see it
Because of the rain
Just then that piece of something
Shot up in the air
As far as I know that something
Is possibly still up there

Elephant

I tried to paint an Elephant

But he kept moving away

I don't mind painting an Elephant

If only he would stay

That silly Elephant

Spilt it over the floor

So the only thing that I could do

Was go and buy some more

But I'm sad to say

They'd run out of Elephant Grey.

The Salesman said I've something else I think

I've lots and lots of Elephant Pink

So I painted another Elephant pink all day

But when the Elephant painted grey

Saw the Elephant of pink

They said My God we've had too much to drink.

Robin Hood

Robin Hood was not
A very good shot
Despite what history said
At the Archery Fayre
The target was there
But he shot himself instead

Tigger

Tigger my ginger cat
Somehow got bitten by a rat
So hurt was her pussy pride
She even contemplated suicide
Her pride returned
When in the house
She finally caught a mouse
When she thought that was that
She was bitten by another rat

Jam

I'm warning you Uncle Sam
Beware beware of Jam
It's always there at breakfast and tea
That's how it gets in you see
There is no escape from Jam
It will find you wherever you am
There's that moment of dread
When you find Jam on your bread
No matter where you are
Jam will not be very far
Dam, dam, dam, dam
Jam.

Nose

This man had a big nose
It was as big as a rose
The red spread to his toes
Toes don't smell like a rose
More like cods' roes
Oh I wouldn't like those
I'd like a duck, a cat and crows
Any of those
But toes?

Paddy

My name is Paddy O'Hare
And sometimes I'm not there
Sometime when I feel right
I'll be on the Isle of Wight
If I'm not there I'll be
On the Isle of Innisfree
If I'm not there
I'll be elsewhere
I might also be
In the lovely vale of Tralee
I spend some time in Spain
And then move on again
I keep on moving you see
The police are after me

The Whale

I'd like to buy a Whale
But where are they on sale?
From what I understand
They're rarely seen on land
A Whale must be in a place
With lots and lots of space
I know where he'll be
The sea! That's it, the sea
If he's to be seen
I'll have to buy a submarine
A submarine would cost a lot
I'd have to sell everything I've got
No! No! I won't do that
Instead I'll buy a Pussy-cat

Clever Me

I can tell an Elephant from a Flea
How jolly clever of me
I can tell a mountain from a tram
That's how clever I am
I can tell a pimple from a spot
That's how clever I've got
I can't tell the difference from a Duck
Oh what bad luck

EX-SERVICE ANT.
WIFE, 3 CHILDREN
AND ELEPHANTS LEG
TO SUPPORT.

Hiawatha

Hi! Hiawatha, your brother and your diawughter
Hi! Your tribe are living near the Waatha
When you marry Minne Haha or Mini Tee-hee
What a Ha-ha-tee-hee wedding that will be

Banana

What a fool is the banana
Lots grow in Ghana
The banana lives in
A thick yellow skin
They can't get out
Even if they shout
The only way to reveal you
Someone has to peel you
When you are revealed
Your fate is sealed
Some hungry soul
Will swallow you whole

Daniel

Daniel in the lions' den
Was the luckiest of men
He had learned from some professors
How to give appetite supressors
The very thing to try on
A hungry lion
Every hungry beast
Was given one at least
By acting this way
Daniel was alive the next day

Expel Elephants

Elephant Elephant
Go away
I don't like Elephants that stay
Twenty-four hours is all I can stand
After that they must be banned
It is very well known
That England is an Elephant-free zone
Pussy-cats and Dogs can stay
But Elephants must go away

Ostrigator

How do you cater
For the Ostrigator?
Does he live on land or sea?
What is his animal category?
He's half one and half the other
Is he only one, has he a brother?
If he wants to procreate
He'll need an Ostrigator mate!

CORONATION
Said Prince Charles
When they place
The Crown on his head
I suppose this means
That Mummy's dead

Frog

Froggy Froggy
Croakity croak
Is that how
You speak or spoke?
Why are you so very fond
Of living in a smelly pond
I saw you eat a Dragonfly
If I did that
I'm sure I'd die

The Mouse

There was a teeny weeny Mouse
Lived in a teeny weeny house
He made a teeny weeny hole
In the cellar near the teeny weeny coal
At night he'd come out to have a teeny weeny play
He'd play a teeny weeny sax
Then someone hit him with an axe
It really was an overkill
But for that he'd be with us teeny weeny still

The Bay

I said to the Bay of Tunisia
Have you by chance any Fish in here?
No there's not said the Bay
All the Fish have gone away
I have only got chips
On my dish here.

Sea

I was walking by the sea
When it splashed me
People with wet trousers
Are not welcome in people's houses
They might laugh at me
But I'll blame it on the sea
See?

Lion

Said a man from Syon
Can you measure me for a Lion?
My inside leg is thirty-two
Said the salesman, that will never do
We haven't got that size Lion
Would you like an Elephant to try on?
No, an Elephant's too big for me
My waist is only thirty-three
Perhaps you'd like to try on a Gnu?
Yes, I think that will do!
Yes, he fits me perfectly
I'll take him to a Zebra tea

Quasimodo

Quasimodo I can tell
That name rings a bell
He rings it in the Notre Dame
He rings it wherever he am
Esmerelda was the love of Quasi
But he was not good-looking was he?

Lesic Lokit Lee

The Lesic Lokit Lee
Will be the death of me
The Lesic Lokit Lee
Is very hard to see
It attacks your head
When you're lying in bed
I foiled the Lesic Lokit Lee
By staying awake you see!

I Dreamed

I dreamed that I was somewhere else, but where?
I looked around but nobody was there!
While I was somewhere else with little to do
So I added one plus one and it came to two
Next I met a little man who had passed on
I often wonder where is, or where he had gone
I awoke one morning at the break of day
The morning was sunlit and sublime
So then I hadn't been somewhere else
I'd been here all the time

Twit

James Warrington Wit
Was an upper-class twit
Why it's hard to say
An upper-class yob
Without a job
A layabout all day
He lay about in Chatham
Lewisham as well
He lay about in Clapham
As to why it is hard to tell
James Warrington Wit
Didn't care a bit
What other people said
And went this way
All his life they say
Until the day he was dead

Family

Oh dear Oh dear
My mum is so fat
She wears huge knickers
And that is that

Yet my dad
Is very thin
The letterbox is
How he gets in

My brother Jim
Is six foot seven
Sees Angel feet
Up in heaven

My sister Sue
Is very small
I trod on her in the hall

Oh dear Oh dear
Oh dearie me
What a strange family

More Jam

I hate Jam
I don't want it to know where I am
I want a Jam-free life
Never letting Jam on my knife
Beware of Jam my friend
It can spread from end to end
Eating Jam is a sin
Letting all that Jam go in
Let your life be pure like me
Totally, totally, Jam free
Be careful my friend
Or Jam will get you in the end

The Gingerbread Boy

Once upon a time there was a baker man and his wife. They lived in a little mill by a stream full of fish and fat frogs. It was all very lovely, *but* the baker and his wife were very, *very* unhappy – do you know why? Well they didn't have any children.

'Oh, I *wish* I had a little boy all of my own.'

When the baker saw his wife crying, he said, 'Don't cry, wife. I will try and get us a little boy.'

So that night, he went to the bakery and said to himself, 'If we can't have a real baby, I'll make one.' So – he got a big bag of white flour and he mixed it with water until it was a big ball of dough – it looked like a big snowball – then he took a jar of ginger and mixed it into the dough. All night he worked, and do you know what he was doing? He was making a gingerbread boy. He made the legs, then the arms, the body, and last he made the gingerbread boy's head. Do you know how he made the eyes? How would you make the gingerbread boy's eyes? Well, this is how the baker made them: he got two currants and popped them in, then he made a little heart out of peppermint and put it inside the body.

When it was all ready he put the gingerbread boy into the oven to make him nice and warm. After a little while the miller heard a tiny voice. 'Let me out, let me out. It's hot in here!' Do you know who it was saying it? The gingerbread boy! Quickly, the miller took him out of the oven and he saw the gingerbread boy was alive!

'Hello, my boy,' said the miller.

'Who are *you?*' said the gingerbread boy.

'I am your daddy.' And he picked him up and kissed him.

Then the little gingerbread boy said, 'What is my name?' The miller said, 'I don't know yet. I will take you home and ask your mother.'

'Oh, let's hurry,' said the gingerbread boy, and off they ran to the miller's house. When his wife opened the door and she saw the gingerbread boy she was so happy she clapped her hands with joy. 'At last! At last I have a little boy all of my own. I shall call him "Gingy" because he is a ginger colour.'

Next morning they took Gingy to start school. At first Gingy was very happy in school, but then one day a naughty boy called Tommy bit Gingy on the arm. 'Oh!' said poor Gingy and Tommy said, 'You taste like a bit of gingerbread,' and he bit poor Gingy again.

The poor little gingerbread boy started to run home – oh dear – it started to rain and he started to get all soggy, and when he arrived home he was just a big ball of dough, like he first was.

When his mother saw him she started to cry and cry. 'Boo-hoo-hoo, what has happened to my poor boy.' And her tears came running down all over gingerbread boy.

'Please don't cry all over me, or I'll fall into little pieces,' said Gingy.

'Come here. I'll make you all better again,' said the baker, and he squeezed all the rain out of gingerbread boy and made him back into a proper boy again.

That night, when they tucked him into bed, gingerbread boy said, 'Mummy, why do I crumple away when it rains?' So mummy had to tell him – he was made of gingerbread, and he was not the same as the other girls and boys.

That night little gingerbread boy was very sad. He didn't want to be just made of bread – he wanted to be made of skin.

'I'm going to run away.' So he put on his clothes and took three apples and two oranges in a bag and off he tramped into the forest behind the house. It was dark as black, and a big owl said, 'Where are *yoo* going *tooo*?'

'Please owl, I'm cold and tired and hungry. Can I shelter under your wing?'

'Oh, all right,' said the owl.

Underneath the wing it was nice and warm, and gingerbread boy went fast asleep. When he woke up it was morning and the owl said, 'I must be off now. I'm going to bed.' And away he flew to bed – because owls don't sleep at night, only in the daytime.

Now gingerbread boy was alone again and he walked through the woods till he came to the top of a hill – and there he saw the house. It was a very funny house – it didn't have any windows, only lots and lots of doors. Gingerbread boy knocked at one door, and out came a funny old man wearing a long blue shirt and no trousers.

'What do you want?' he said.

'I'm hungry,' said gingerbread boy, 'and I'm cold.'

The old man took him inside. 'I'll soon have you warm. Just get into this nice bath of hot water.'

Splash. In jumped gingerbread boy. 'Oh, this is lovely,' he said, and then a terrible bad thing happened – gingerbread boy started to come to pieces in the hot water. 'Help! Help!' he cried, 'Get me out!' But it was too late.

The funny old man rolled all the pieces into a big ball of dough and put it on the mantlepiece. Next morning the funny old man went to the market and tried to sell the big piece of gingerbread. No one would buy it, but then along came the gingerbread boy's daddy, the baker.

'I need some dough,' he said, so he bought it off the old man for a penny.

Now, the baker didn't *know* it was really the gingerbread boy he had bought but, when he got back to the bakery, he saw the little peppermint heart sticking out of the lump of gingerbread.

'Hooray, I've found my gingerbread boy again!' And quickly,

quickly, he made the gingerbread boy all over again, just like he used to be.

'Oh, daddy, daddy,' said the gingerbread boy. 'I'll never run away again.' And he hugged and kissed him. Just then in came mummy and guess what *she* had – *another* little gingerbread boy.

'This is your new brother,' said daddy. 'When you ran away and we couldn't find you I made *another* little gingerbread boy.'

'Oh, how lovely! Now we can play together.'

And so they did, and they all lived happily ever after.

A Dustbin of Milligan

Porridge

Why is there no monument
   To Porridge in our land?
If it's good enough to eat
   It's good enough to stand!

On a plinth in London
   A statue we should see
Of Porridge made in Scotland
   Signed "Oatmeal, O.B.E."
       (*By a young dog of three*)

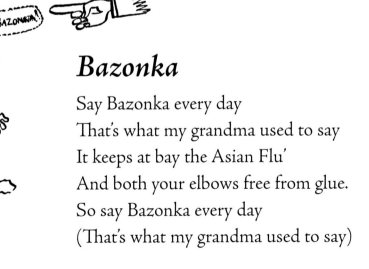

Bazonka

Say Bazonka every day
That's what my grandma used to say
It keeps at bay the Asian Flu'
And both your elbows free from glue.
So say Bazonka every day
(That's what my grandma used to say)

Don't say it if your socks are dry!
Or when the sun is in your eye!
Never say it in the dark
(The word you see emits a spark)
Only say it in the day
(That's what my grandma used to say!)

Young Tiny Tim took her advice.
He said it once, he said it twice
He said it till the day he died
And even after *that* he tried
To say Bazonka! every day
Just like my grandma used to say.

Now folks around declare it's true
That every night at half past two
If you'll stand upon your head
And shout Bazonka! from your bed
You'll hear the word as clear as day
Just like my grandma used to say!

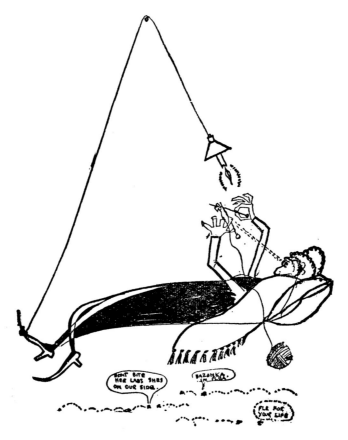

Lady B's Fleas.

Lady Barnaby takes her ease
Knitting overcoats for fleas
By this kindness, fleas are smitten
Thats why she's _very_ _rarely_ bitten.

Why?

American Detectives
　　Never remove their hats
When investigating murders
　　In other people's flats.

P.S. Chinese Tecs
　　Are far more dreaded!
　　And they always appear
　　　bare-headed!

"Gentlemen – a clue – this
man recently had his trousers
in the press."
SH

Mrs. Dighty

Mrs. Dighty
In her nightie
Walking in the dark

Trod upon
A puppy dog's tail
And made the creature bark

Mrs. Dighty
In her nightie
Let the puppy go

By lifting up
  her instep
And raising her
  big toe.

Holes

Mountains should have holes in
    To see to the other side.
By observing the view thru this aperture
    Would save a considerable ride.

So Fair is She

So fair is she!
So fair her face
So fair her pulsing figure

Not so fair
The maniacal stare
Of a husband who's much bigger.

Illness Is Good For You

One good appendicitis—
  Or a cure for St. Vitus dance
Pays for a Harley Street Surgeon's
  Vacation in the South of France.

Nelson

'Tis due to pigeons
  that alight
On Nelson's hat
  that makes it white.

Soldier Freddy
          was never ready,
But Soldier Neddy,
     unlike Freddy,
Was always ready
          and steady,

Thats why,
When soldier Neddy
Is outside Buckingham Palace on guard in the
          pouring wind and rain
          being steady and ready,
     Freddie —
          is home in beddy

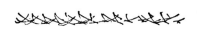

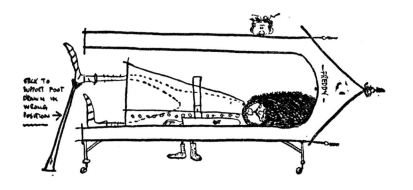

Scorflufus

By a well-known National Health Victim No. 3908631

There are many diseases,
That strike people's kneeses,
Scorflufus! is one by name
It comes from the East
Packed in bladders of yeast
So the Chinese must take half the blame.

There's a case in the files
Of Sir Barrington-Pyles
While hunting a fox one day
Shot up in the air
And *remained hanging there!*
While the hairs on his socks turned grey!

Aye! Scorflufus had struck!
At man, beast and duck.
And the knees of the world went Bong!
Some knees went Ping!
Other knees turned to string
From Balham to old Hong-Kong.

Should you hold your life dear,
Then the remedy's clear,
If you're offered some yeast – don't eat it!
Turn the offer down flat–
Don your travelling hat–
Put an egg in your boot – and beat it!

A Witch's Tale

The Witch!

Once upon a time there was a little boy and girl, the girl was called Mary and the little boy was called Tommy. One day, as they were on their way home, they saw an *old* woman with a *long* black cloak and *long* pointed ginger boots and a white face with purple eyes and a long pointed nose.

She said, 'Hello little children, won't you buy one of my nice packets of bubble soap?'

And they said, 'No, we haven't any money.'

She said, 'Never mind little children: have one for nothing,' and she held out a large packet of yellow powder. 'Put it in your bath,' she said, 'It will make the whole bath full of lovely yellow bubbles.'

So, the children took this yellow powder, and that night they emptied *all* the yellow powder in. All of a sudden a terrible thing happened! They felt themselves getting *smaller* and *smaller* and smaller! They got so small that when their mummy came to empty the bath, she couldn't see them. She pulled the plug out and the children went right down the drain, down and down, down *right* under the ground! It was dark *very* dark. They were shouting 'Help! help! help!' but their voices were *so* tiny no one could hear them. Then they saw a little speck of light in the distance, and they knew they were coming near the end of the drain. There was a terrible sound of roaring water and then *pop*! and out they popped.

They found themselves in a big wide stream in the countryside. They grabbed hold of a brown leaf that was floating by and pulled themselves on. (Now what do you think made the children get so small? The powder? Yes, it was a *magic* yellow powder.)

Suddenly, a great shadow fell across the children and a long thin hand reached out towards them. They heard a terrible cackling sound. 'He, he, he, he, he, he, he, he,' and they saw a great white face and they saw she had long pointed ginger boots – it was the old woman who gave them the yellow powder. What was she? She was a witch. 'He, he, he, he, he,' she said, 'Got you!' and popped them into a glass pickle jar. She jumped on a broomstick and *flew* up into the sky. Up and up and up she went until she came to a great black cloud full of thunder. She flew round and round the cloud and screamed a magic word, 'Yimbon balla boo-yim-bon balla boo.' And a great door in the side of the cloud opened. In she flew, for inside the cloud was a great red witch's palace, all made of glass and animal bones. She took them into a great room, full of frogs.

She put them on a table and the little boy said, 'What are you going to do with us?'

She said, 'I'm going to turn you into a pair of black Giant-boots,' and she made a magic pass and said some secret words, 'Tip-a-tip a Par-par Ti-po-tee-O-Yiggerely-Jiggereley – one two three!'

Fhooshhhhh! The children disappeared in a cloud of orange and mauve smoke and in their place was a pair of black Giant-boots. The poor children had been changed into boots!

Just then, there was a great knocking on the door, Bom-Bom-Bom! The Witch said, 'Who is there?'...And a great voice said, 'It's Giant Jim...have you got my black Giant-boots ready...?'

'Yes, I have, he, he, he,' she said.

Are they made of children?' he said.

'Yes they are,' said the witch.

'*Good*,' he said, 'I like my boots to be made of children,' and he sat down and tried them on. 'Oh they fit me fine, how much?'

The Giant.

She said, 'I don't want money. I want you to catch me a Kangaroo, because I want to have Kangaroo tail stew!'

The Giant was puzzled. He said, 'Er what's a Kangaroo?'

(What is a Kangaroo children? What does a Kangaroo do – hops?).

The Witch said, 'Go to Australia, there're *plenty* of Kangaroos there.'

(Are there Kangaroos in Australia? No, yes.) So that's where Giant Jim went. He was so tall he only had to take three paces to get from England to Australia, and there he was, Giant Jim in the middle of the Australian Desert.

Now this Giant was very stupid. He couldn't remember his name. He said, 'Oh my name is – er – Giant Tom? Er – dat's right, my name's Giant Tom, isn't it? Oh Giant Jim? dat's right, my name's Giant Tom, isn't it? Oh Giant Jim? Oh Taarrr, my name is Giant…er Jim. I've come to Australia to look for a er… er…Elephant, no no no not an Elephant…ah a Kangaroo… dat's it.' So he kept an eye open for a Kangaroo.

Soon along came a Kangaroo. And his name was Fred Fertanggggg. His name was Fred Fertanggg. He was called that because when he hopped he went Fertang! Fertang! Fertang!

The Giant saw him and grabbed him. 'Got him! I've caught a Kangaroo. Hooray!'

Now, you remember that little Mary and Tom were the Giant's boots? So Mary said, 'Let's pinch his feet so he has to take us off,' so they *squeezed* and *squeezed* until the boots hurt his feet so much he shouted. 'Oh my feet, oh my poor old tootsies. Oh these boots are too small. I'll take 'em off.' He was so angry he went back to the Witch's palace in the clouds and he said, 'I want a new pair of boots, these are too small. Look at my poor tootsies, they're going doing-doing.'

She said, 'Have you got the Kangaroo yet?'

He said, 'I'm not giving it to you until you make these boots bigger.'

She said, 'Oh dear it means I'll have to change the boots back into children, then I'll have to make the children bigger and then I'll turn them into bigger boots.' She took the boots into her room and she threw a magic red and green powder at them. And, the boots turned back into Mary and Tommy again. 'Now,' she said, 'Now where's that orange powder.' And, as she turned her back to get it, the children ran out of the room and slammed the door.

Outside, the giant said, 'Oh! who are you?'

They said, 'The Witch sent us out to look after your Kangaroo while you go and get your new boots.'

'Oh,' he said, 'O.K.! hold him,' and he gave them Fred Fertangggg.

As soon as he'd gone, the children jumped into the Kangaroo's pocket and said, 'Hop it…or we'll all be killed.' Off hopped Fred Fertang, Fertang! Fertang! Fertang!

He kept hopping till they were far away in a big forest full of great brown trees that reached up almost to the sky.

Inside it was all dark, and Tommy said to Mary, 'We'll be safe here from the Witch and the Giant; it's too dark for them to see us.'

But right behind them they heard the crashing sound of the Giant. He was pulling all the trees up. And up above they could hear the Witch flying on her broomstick saying 'After them, after them, ha, ha, ha, ha.'

The Giant was getting very close…closer…closer! But just then Fred Fertang saw a little tiny hole in a tree. Fertang hopped inside. Inside the tree was a little tiny room with a tiny little yellow light in the middle. At a little table sat a little goblin with a red hat, trousers, pink jacket and purple and white boots.

'Who are you?' said the children.

'My name is Oggley Poogley, I'm the keeper of the Gentle Dragon.'

'Oh please help us Oggley Poogley. There's a Giant called Jim after us; he's pulling up all the trees.'

'Pulling up all the trees,' said Oggley Poogley looking very angry and waggling his eyebrows. 'He mustn't do that, these trees are Dragon's food. I'll soon stop him.' And he went outside, looked up at the Giant and said, 'Hey you, stop pulling up those trees.'

The Giant said, 'No I won't. You want to fight?'

The goblin said, 'No, I'm too small, but I'll get you a fight.' And he took a little blue whistle and he blew it. Then there was a terrible noise from inside the forest. A great crashing, and through the trees came the Goblin's Dragon. He was as tall as ten houses, and covered in thick red skin with purple stripes; he had a mouth full of sharp teeth like knives. When the Giant saw him, he was frightened; he let out a yell, 'Help, help,' and he started to run away. The Dragon chased him and breathed a great stream of flames at him and he set the Giant's trousers on fire. 'Oh help,' he shouted, and all his trousers were burnt at the back and his shirt tail was hanging out.

Then the goblin blew his whistle and the Dragon came back. 'Don't be frightened of him,' said the goblin. 'He won't hurt, he's a *good* Dragon.'

'Oh please help us, we want to be big like we were before the Witch turned us into midgets,' said the children.

'Oh,' said the goblin. 'There's only one person who could do that. He's the Great Wizard called Bongg. He lives in an Eagle's nest at the top of a great Silver Palace right up the mighty snow mountains.'

'How do we get there,' said the children.

'Well,' said the goblin. 'You'd better jump in Fred Fertang's

pocket again and tell him to follow the forest road until he gets
to the Milk River. When you arrive there you will see an old
Yellow Owl wearing trousers and a school cap: ask him what
to do.'

Before they went he gave them a golden pebble. 'If ever you
want me,' he said, 'rub this on your hand.'

So, off they went in Fred Fertang's pocket. Fertang! Fertang!
Fertang! Fertang! The sun was going down when they arrived
at the Great Milk River. It was all milk, and, all along the
banks, pussy cats were drinking from it. But there was *no* sign
of the owl. 'Twit-two whit.' They looked up, and *there* he was,
in a tree, wearing a shirt and a school cap.

'You looking for me?'

'Yes we are,' said the children. 'Oggley Poogley, the goblin,
said you would show us the way across the Milk River to meet
the Great Wizard called Bong!'

'Oh yes,' said the owl. 'You'll have to go part of the way by
Flying Pussy Cat.' And he pointed to a great white pussy cat
with a propeller on the end of his tail. 'Get on my back,' said
the cat. They all jumped into his fur. 'Hold tight,' said the cat.
The propeller on his tail started to go round and round. Up
and up he flew, over the Milk River, over the houses, over the
trees and the lakes.

Down below they could see trees with chocolate apples
growing on them. 'Oh, I'd like one of those,' said Fred Fertang,

the Kangaroo, so, the pussy cat flew *very* low, and, as they went over the trees, they all grabbed a chocolate apple. On and *on* they flew!

Suddenly, the cat's propeller stopped. 'Oh, help,' he said. 'Help, we're falling, something's wrong! My tail's run out of petrol.' Down and down they came, faster and *faster* and FASTER. *Crash...*! Luckily, they all fell on to a big hay cart. Whee dong! whee dong! whee donggg! All three landed safely.

'Oo's that in there,' said a voice. It was the driver of the hay cart. 'Come out of there or I'll poke you with my stick.' Pokey, pokey, pokey. They all crawled out.

'What are you doing in there,' he said.

'We're looking for the Wizard called Bong,' said Tommy.

'Oh, dear,' he said. 'That's a dangerous journey. I'll take you as far as I can, so you'd better have a sleep.' So they fell off to sleep.

All night long they slept in the cart, and soon it started to snow. 'All right, you three get off here,' said the cart driver. They all jumped down. 'Mind how you go. There're terrible dangers ahead for you all. Good luck!' and off he went.

The children jumped into Fred Fertang's pocket and up the snowy road

The Wizard.

he hopped. Fertang. Fertang. Fertang. Oh it was cold, all their noses went red. They saw a big sign:

BEWARE OF THE DANGEROUS WHITE RABBIT.

They thought, 'That's funny, how can a rabbit be dangerous?'

'Who said dat?' said a voice from a hole in the ground, and out popped a white rabbit.

'Are you the dangerous white rabbit?' they asked.

'Yes, I'm the dangerous white rabbit,' he said.

'Why are you dangerous?' asked the children.

'I eat grass, I'm dangerous to grass. Now, where are you all going?' said the White Rabbit.

'We are going to see the Wizard called Bong.'

'Oh, I've always wanted to meet him, can I come too?' said the Rabbit. So into Fred Fertang's pocket he popped.

As they turned a bend in the road, there in the middle was a great Tiger. *Grr.* He sprang at them, and swallowed them all up, *Gulp.* And there they were, Mary, Tommy, Fred Fertang and the White Rabbit, all inside the Tiger's tummy.

It was very dark inside the Tiger's tummy. Only when the Tiger opened his mouth to growl did the light get in. 'Don't worry,' said the White Rabbit, 'I've got some matches and a candle.' So he lit a candle. He held the candle up, and all the smoke started to go round the Tiger's tummy and made him feel ill. Oh he felt so sick. All his stripes fell off. The candle started to burn his tummy and he started to cough and cough and cough. Hugh *Cough, cough…coughhh.* And he coughed so much he coughed out all the children, the Kangaroo and the Rabbit. And while he was still coughing, Tommy rubbed the golden pebble that the goblin gave him and made a wish. There was a rush of wind, and a strange sound, Hoing! A little blue light appeared in the sky. It came rushing down, there was a flash, and a puff of smoke. And there was a Giant Black Man.

'I am the slave of the golden pebble, whatever you ask me to do, I will do.'

'Please can you take us to the Palace of the Wizard called Bong?'

'Your wish is my command.' He clapped his hands. And there was a flying carpet. 'Jump on that carpet and it will take you to his Palace.'

On they jumped and up went the carpet, flying through the sky. And the carpet went so fast that the wind nearly blew them off. Faster and faster they went. And there down below, on top of a snowy mountain, they saw a Silver Palace.

'That's the Wizard's Castle,' said White Rabbit, and the magic carpet started to go down and down and down. And they got slower and slower. As they were flying over the roof of the Wizard's Castle, they heard a terrible cackling. 'He! he! he!' and there flying above them, was the Witch!

'I'll have you now,' she said. But the magic carpet flew through the window of the Wizard's Castle and landed on the floor, right by the Wizard's bed. He was fast asleep. When he heard the noise, he woke up.

'Oh dear, dear, dear, what's going on?' he said.

'There's a black Witch after us,' said the White Rabbit.

'Oh, we'll soon fix her,' said the Wizard called Bong. He picked up a big gun, full of mud, and he fired it at her. And Splosh! It hit her right in the face. Down she came, *Splash*! right in the big lake.

'Now,' said the Wizard called Bong. 'What's the trouble?'

'Please can you make us like ordinary size children again?'

'Yes,' said the Magician. 'Now, all stand against that wall and close your eyes.' He took a long glass rod with a star on the end, and he tapped the children on the nose. And bong-bong-bong-veroom, they went back to their own size again.

'Now, off you go home,' said Bong the Wizard.

They all jumped on to the magic carpet, and up in the sky they went. But, the Witch, she was waiting for them. After she'd fallen in the water, she changed herself into a cloud of smoke. So, when the children saw her, they didn't know it was her.

'Oh, look,' said the Rabbit. 'There's a smoke cloud following us.'

A little bird flew over them. 'Be careful of that smoke, it's the Witch,' he cried.

So Mary and Tommy got a paper bag, and they waited till the

smoke cloud was very near, then they popped it over the smoke and caught it all in the bag.

And they could hear her inside the bag shouting. 'Let me out, let me out, let me out!'

But they didn't let her out, and the magic carpet went faster and faster, up, up, up into the clouds, and there they were, flying through the clouds back home.

When they got home, their Mummy and Daddy were so pleased to see them, and the White Rabbit and Fred Fertang and Tommy and Mary lived happily ever after.

But what happened to the Witch? She's *still* inside the paper bag! He! He! He!

Silly Verse
for Kids

Look at all those monkeys

Look at all those monkeys
Jumping in their cage.
Why don't they all go out to work
And earn a decent wage?

How can you say such silly things,
Are you a son of mine?
Imagine monkeys travelling on
The Morden-Edgware line!

But what about the Pekinese!
They have an allocation.
'Don't travel during Peke hour,'
It says on every station.

My Gosh, you're right, my clever boy,
I never thought of that!
And so they left the monkey house,
While an elephant raised his hat.

Tell me little woodworm

Tell me little woodworm
Eating thru the wood.
Surely all that sawdust
Can't do you any good.

Heavens! Little woodworm
You've eaten all the chairs
So *that's* why poor old Grandad's
Sitting outside on the stairs.

Hipporhinostricow

Such a beast is the Hipporhinostricow
How it got so mixed up we'll never know how;
It sleeps all day, and whistles all night,
And it wears yellow socks which are far too tight.

If you laugh at the Hipporhinostricow,
You're bound to get into an awful row;
The creature is protected you see
From silly people like you and me.

Said the General

Said the General of the Army,
'I think that war is barmy'
So he threw away his gun:
Now he's having much more fun.

Granny

Through every nook and every cranny
The wind blew in on poor old Granny;
Around her knees, into each ear
(And up her nose as well, I fear).

All through the night the wind grew worse,
It nearly made the vicar curse.
The top had fallen off the steeple
Just missing him (and other people).

It blew on man, it blew on beast.
It blew on nun, it blew on priest.
It blew the wig off Auntie Fanny –
But most of all, it blew on Granny ! !

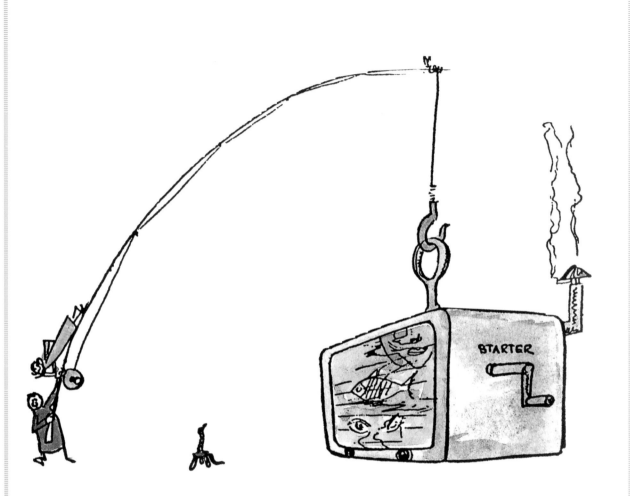

Today I saw a little worm

Today I saw a little worm
Wriggling on his belly.
Perhaps he'd like to come inside
And see what's on the Telly.

Teeth

English Teeth, English Teeth!
Shining in the sun
A part of British heritage
Aye, each and every one.

English Teeth, Happy Teeth!
Always having fun
Clamping down on bits of fish
And sausages half done.

English Teeth! HEROES' Teeth!
Hear then click! and clack!
Let's sing a song of praise to them –
Three Cheers for the Brown Grey
    and Black.

Can a parrot

Can a parrot
Eat a carrot
Standing on his head?
If I did that my mum would
    send me
Straight upstairs to bed.

I'm not frightened of Pussy Cats

I'm not frightened of Pussy Cats
They only eat up mice and rats,
But a Hippopotamus
Could eat the Lotofus!

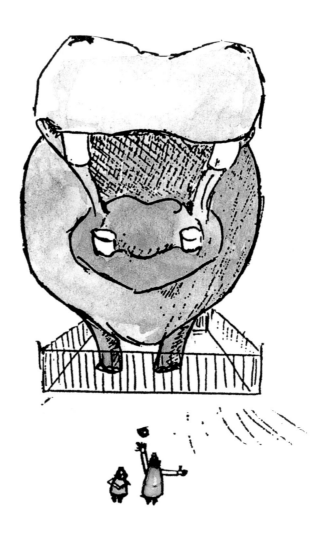

Down the stream the swans all glide

Down the stream the swans all glide;
It's quite the cheapest way to ride.
Their legs get wet,
Their tummies wetter:
I think after all
The bus is better.

On the Ning Nang Nong

On the Ning Nang Nong
Where the Cows go Bong!
And the Monkeys all say Boo!
There's a Nong Nang Ning
Where the trees go Ping!
And the tea pots Jibber Jabber Joo.

On the Nong Ning Nang
All the mice go Clang!
And you just can't catch 'em when they do!
So it's Ning Nang Nong!
Cows go Bong!
Nong Nang Ning!
Trees go Ping!
Nong Ning Nang!
The mice go Clang!
What a noisy place to belong,
Is the Ning Nang
   Ning Nang Nong!!

My sister Laura

My sister Laura's bigger than me
And lifts me up quite easily.
I can't lift her, I've tried and tried;
She must have something heavy inside.

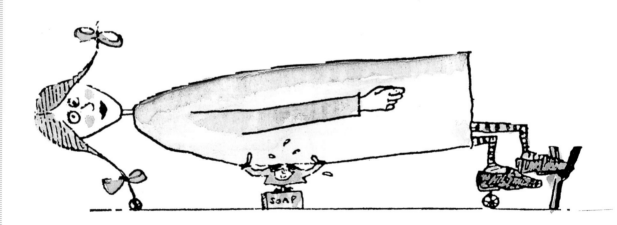

The ABC

T'was midnight in the schoolroom
And every desk was shut,
When suddenly from the alphabet
Was heard a loud 'Tut-tut!'

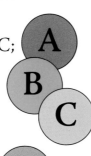

Said A to B, 'I don't like C;
His manners are a lack.
For all I ever see of C
Is a semi-circular back!'

'I disagree,' said D to B,
'I've never found C so.
From where I stand, he seems to be
An uncompleted O.'

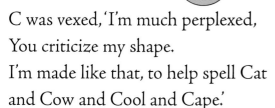

C was vexed, 'I'm much perplexed,
You criticize my shape.
I'm made like that, to help spell Cat
and Cow and Cool and Cape.'

'He's right,' said E; said F,
'Whoopee!'
Said G, ''Ip, 'ip, 'ooray!'
'You're dropping me,' roared H to G.
'Don't do it please I pray!'

'Out of my way,' LL said to K
'I'll make poor I look ILL.'
To stop this stunt, J stood in front,
And presto! ILL was JILL.

'U know,' said V, 'that W
Is twice the age of me,
For as a Roman V is five
I'm half as young as he.'

X and Y yawned sleepily,
'Look at the time!' they said.
'Let's all get off to beddy byes.'
They did, then 'Z-z-z.'

or

alternative last verse

X and Y yawned sleepily,
'Look at the time!' they said.
They all jumped in to beddy byes
And the last one in was Z!

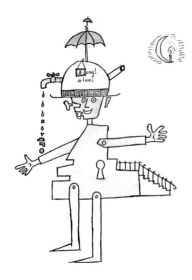

Bump!

Things that go 'bump!' in the night,
Should not really give one a fright.
It's the hole in each ear
That lets in the fear,
That, and the absence of light!

Rain

There are holes in the sky
Where the rain gets in,
But they're every so small
That's why rain is thin.

Index